Sacred & Sacrosanct
a collection of poems

William Forchion

Dreamcatcher Entertainment
Brattleboro, Vermont
05301

William Forchion

Published by:

Dreamcatcher Entertainment

72 Cotton Mill Hill #100

Brattleboro, VT 05301

www.dreamcatcherfilmworks.com

info@dreamcatcherfilmworks.com

ISBN: 0-9982978-2-8

ISBN-13: 978-0-9982978-2-8

DEDICATION

Zeb, Quin and Evalina thank you for being you.

M.M thank you for your strategic help.

EMF thank you for the push.

CONTENTS

Introduction

Until recently I had not considered the word sacrosanct. I had held the understanding that when something was sacred it was held in the highest regard. Now I have discovered sacrosanct which by definition is something that is extremely sacred, to be held in a regard higher than sacred. I had not considered that there could be more than sacred. My mind is opening to the idea of what is beyond sacred what more there can be. What does extremely sacred look like? feel like? The idea of beyond sacred, the reality of beyond sacred rocks my physical world and my spiritual world. In my travels I have been to sacred places in Australia, Asia, Europe and the U.S., experiencing awe and wonder. I now feel that I am being welcomed to discover sacrosanct places. As I discover the sacrosanct around me I am open to discover the sacrosanct inside me. Just as I was drawn to find the definition of sacrosanct, something deep within me needs me to find sacrosanct places in the physical world to connect with my sacrosanct soul.

Today

No one warned me about today, or
yesterday, for that matter.
I wonder about tomorrow, yet cannot
put much energy to it because I first
must manage today.
Was I told that life might get in the way
of living?
Did someone ever say the chemicals that
make you wonderful could one day
drive you mad?
It is today.
I am the same and yet so very different
than what I once was.
When did the gravity of life increase to
nearly crushing?
When did I become too weak to stand
under the weight of living?
When did I start considering giving up?
When did okay become okay?
And striving for wonderful left to
others?
When did I forget how to breathe?
No one warned me about today or
yesterday, for that matter.

I FLY

With this ring I thee wed, I FLY.
The honeymoon is over, I FLY.
Three children born in just under a
decade, I FLY.
Babies cry our love is torn.
This is where papas run and daddies
stay.
I'm a Daddy. I FLY.
Figuring out how we love again, I FLY.
You forget me and you see him, I FLY.
So many sorrys, so many forgives, too
much to forget, I FLY.
You return to us and leave your heart
with him, I FLY.
Your eyes no longer see me. I FLY.
I pack my bags and walk through the
door you left open, I FLY.
It is not from you I run.
It is to you I want to run.
You are no longer there. I FLY.
Whatever tomorrow holds, whether it is
Us, it is You, it is Me, I do not know.
I do know I Forever Love YOU.
I FLY.

Truth

My eyes well with tears for my truth
looks like no one else's.
validation, respect, purpose can be
looked for and never found until within
I find it and match it to that.
Unique does not come in degrees.
no matter how hard I fix my gaze I can
never see myself, I must know myself
unseen.
yet, we are taught to accept nothing we
can not see.
Truth is a matter of perspective and no
two of us has the same perspective.
My truth is also untrue.
and my eyes well with tears.
and my tears stain my face.
and my soul shivers inside seeking
comfort.

Enough

You are enough.

You were born perfect.

And then someone told you to try
harder.

You heard your shape was not the same
as some others.

Your skin is too fair, too dark, to
freckled, too plain.

You could be smarter.

You make someone else feel dumb.

Somewhere we forgot to wash our
hands of this.

And our hands soiled the rest of us,
until we began to swallow the filth
without question.

It is time to forget.

It is time to remember:

> *mistakes are learning in process.
> *you can be no one else but you.

*your uniqueness is what makes
you special.
*there is nothing wrong with
being special.
*the downs are there to
emphasize how wonderful the
ups are.
*and the in between is neither up
nor down.
When I say "You" I more often mean
"I".
I was born perfect.
I am enough.

Human

Today is the day.

today is the only day.

I am being who I am meant to be.

I am not a human doing.

I am a human being.

Ghost

So many seek happiness
chasing it
refusing to let go of hurt, pain, fear
unable to grasp, with hands full
happiness eludes
unable to settle for that which can not be
found
so many seek happiness
not knowing how afraid they are of
wanting joy
not believing they are entitled
not realizing the only thing keeping
them from knowing joy
is the daily bath in fear
all too often it takes more than wanting
there is a divine knowing in knowing
we are worthy of this we need
within each we must know it is ours
we are worthy
we are worth it
before we do anything to get it
we must be and be fully
it is our being that owns it

only words

I wonder what would happen if I could
always use the perfect set of words?
could I make everyone love me?
would I always be happy?
would everything I wished for suddenly
come to me?
If the right words always flew from my
mouth would there always be someone
to listen at my side?
would my head swell then explode with
pride?
would I become pompous, boastful,
smug?
I hope you would be there to hear me
ask for a hug?

Self same

Self, selfish, selfless, explaining self, discovering self. Who am I? How do I answer the question? Do I answer with what it is I do? Or do I answer with what I have done? Or do I answer with what it is I am capable of? I am amazing. Is that really who I am? I am horrible. I am capable of anything I set my mind to do. So, therefore I constantly seek to broaden my mind. I seek to expand my capabilities. My seeking is not because I feel lacking. My seeking is because I have longing. I long for more. I long to be more connected. I long to be more creative. I long to be wiser. I long to experience more amazing. With all my longing I do not long to do more. I long to be more, more aware, more present, more open, more me. I long to continue evolving. I long to continue becoming me. So, who am I? I am a human being actively engaged in the process of being.

un - knowing

I have crossed the threshold into the
place of unknowing.
A place I did not know existed yet fear
arriving at.
My fears were unfounded
Fearing neither drove me nearer or
away from here.
And here I am without fear unknowing
the unknowable.
Accepting the information that seems to
cease upon knowing.
Here I find myself uncomfortably
comfortable
as my mind urges me to run
my feet root themselves to clouds.
I long to be bamboo in the wind.
As I long for wind.
For if there was something to resist I
could train myself not to resist.

In this place of unknowing all that I
once knew seems a lie.
My before has become someone else's
memory.
My now is a reflection of what never
was that strives not to be.
I long for the threshold
not to go back to know from where I
came.
I seek to enjoy,
yet that which I seek ceases in the
seeking.
Here in the place of unknowing,
I learn to un-know and accept that as
knowing.

If I replaced you with I

What power you have
with your smile you hold back an army
of sadness.
your hope dams a river of despair.
your uncertainty does not allow
frustration a firm footing.
your tears are not weakness but strength
to purge.
What power you have
to bend to the breaking point and return
to upright.
to think what has been un-thought
before
and know it will come to be.
your tears wash away the years of
untruths to reveal the true you.
What power you have
to stop being what you have been told
to be in order to be who you are meant
to be.

another day

Today is earth day.
Stop. Don't look at your watch or check
the calendar.
Today is earth day.
You live on this earth and today is a
day.
So why is one day a special day to clean
up?
three hundred and sixty four days I am
allowed to walk past trash with a clean
conscience.
and one day I can tidy up a little and
cleanse my guilt.
I refuse that reality because, today is
earth day.
Oh yesterday was also and tomorrow
will be again.
It is not my job to fix what someone else
broke.
It is my job to not let it stay broke If I
want it to work.
This is my earth
This is my day.
For as long as I live it will be that way.

Only

it is not that I don't fit in
or that I stand out.
It is that I am different
not so different as to attract attention
yet different enough to overlook.
from one perspective I might be unique
from another I may be so similar to
everything as to conform into nothing.
from my perspective this is me
explaining me only proves to confuse
you and me
therefore I am content to just be.

Perfect

Before they spoke my name
I existed in a place where words had no
meaning
Everything existed on purpose
We were all connected
Each of us was all of us
and all of us were unique
For without each individual there could
be no whole
what is now called living was once
called flowing
my being explained my doing
and my doing did not define me
words now cross my lips
meanings cloud my mind
my doing confuses my being
when I emerged into this world
this piece became the whole
separated from the all
all became unclear
the flow forgot to flow
words were needed to define
meanings became necessary to explain
it all seemed to happen
when they spoke my name.

The power of words

Sticks and stones may break my bones
but words can never hurt me.
This resonated poorly with me as a child
and still resonates poorly with me.
Long before I had heard this saying my
soul had been nearly crushed by a word.
As a result I feared words. I did not
want to wield them clumsily and
possibly crush someone else's soul. As I
grew older I also discovered we
individually place weight on words, we
individually add power or meaning to
words. I can give a word the power to
destroy me. I can also give power to a
word to buoy me out of the depths of
despair. Which makes me question Do
the words actually have power? Or is
the power added by each of us as we
receive? Do we empower the words to
harm us? Do we empower the words to
strengthen us? We have to answer these
question for our self, individually.
While I work toward my answers I will
purposefully work to put together
words that educate, empower and
entertain. And I will infuse my words
with the essence of my soul.

Who am I?

I am opening to the awareness that I am
the Fool. Blindly moving through life
using feeling rather than sight to guide
my way. I have fought frustration
considering there may be another way
and remaining blind to the alternatives.
I may not have witnessed the fingers
pointing in confusion or the looks of
disdain and disgust. I have been all to
aware of the mocking laughter and the
hand hidden sniggers. And I have
caught myself, questioning if I should
trust my sightless feeling. Mockery,
disgust, and disdain are not helpful
guides. When I put this aside, when I
leave my detractors where they stand
and do not allow them passage in my
mind it becomes clear. On the blind
journey each moment is a moment of
reaching the goal. Falling down gives
new perspective. Rising up builds
strength. The Fool can be a King. To the
Fool anything is possible. The Fool can
be anything and always return the Fool
and all others can only be what they are.
For in changing from what they are
their existence falls into question. Today
I embrace the Fool who would be King
or anything and still the Fool.

Who am I? (2)

It is easy to describe an elephant by
saying how unlike a horse it is.
And yet that does not describe the
elephant.
Here I stand to explain myself and I
have never seen me.
I have seen my reflection.
I can tell you what I have done.
Some of which I am proud of and some
not so much.
Is that who I am?
Or am I what I do? did? done?
My skin is brown, grayish at times when
it is dry.
My mind wanders.
It has mapped half the galaxy, if I am
not mistaken.
I speak from my heart, no deeper, from
my soul.
And when I hurt it aches to the core of
my soul.
I love fully.
And sometimes that aches to the core of
my soul.
Does any of this even begin to answer
the question?
Maybe the question should never be
asked?

From the moment of birth I have been
evolving.
The infant me was nothing like the
toddler.
The toddler me was nothing like the
little kid.
The little kid was only a shadow of the
teenager.
The teenager to the middle - ager could
most easily be described as upheaval.
I am a being of light and love, darkness
and pain, ambition and hope, vengeance
and rage.
I am unlike anyone or anything other
than me.
I am exactly who I am.

Nothing

I just went to a most amazing place. A place I have feared to go. What I feared was the unknowing of what I would find. I have always known the general vicinity of this place yet did not not know it's exact location. Well, I found it. I so wish to share it with the world and that is impossible. For sharing it destroys it. Sharing it complicates the understanding and awareness of what it is. Today I went nowhere and experienced nothing. Technically I was somewhere but in the moment everything dropped away. Everything dropped away. There was no baggage, no fear, no expectation, no story, no color, no shape, no hope, no desire. Describing nothing is a process of illuminating what isn't there. Everything isn't there. It is calm. That is the only description I have. It is calm. Everything remains at the fringe of this place keeping it in perfect balance, keeping it calm. I have finally given myself permission to enter, however brief, however fleeting in the nothing.

Life

Our souls are placed inside this bubble separated from the oneness that is GOD. For a lifetime we endure with only moments of interconnectedness. Some will find soul mates others will tire, whither and die in the search. We retain hope with the memory of the divine Oneness. We find comfort in the creations of our conjuring. We dream of soaring reconnecting for, one day, we will again.

at the intersection

The revolution begins at the crossroads
where reasonable objection meets moral
obligation.
A place where continuing with the same
is just not bearable any longer.
The revolution begins with a pause
a moment of reflection
possibly a full stop.
When it begins it does not move swiftly.
The movement is calculated.
For turning one hundred eighty degrees
brings one back to the place
that birthed the path, the process that
needs to be turned from.
The revolution should not be an
evolution of the unwanted.
The revolution should be the birth of
something all together new.
A new thing created in love
A creation protected by love
not nurtured in fear, doubt, frustration
or anger.
The revolution begins at the crossroads.
The revolution may be simply staying
put ceasing to move further
along a path that is unfruitful,
unfulfilling, unhealthy.
The revolution might possibly begin
nurturing the charred soil in
preparation

of new growth, new hope, new
possibilities.
The revolution need not be violent.
It need be caring, loving.
The revolution is inside me.
It is also inside you.
It lovingly aches to come out, to be born
in the world.
It yearns to vibrate throughout the
universe as a word, as a song, as an
action.
We will recognize the revolutionaries,
for they will radiate.
They will shine, Oh, they will shine.
The radiance of the revolution will
illuminate even the darkest of places
depositing hope, love.
There will be love in abundance.
Lay down your arms.
Open your mind.
Open your heart.
Each of us was created in love.
This is the crossroads.

Morning

Wake up
Wake up
The dream has become the nightmare
has become the dream.
I got it wrong
A revolution comes full circle
The beginning is the end is the
beginning
A cycle of repetition
The revolution does not bring me some
place new
it brings me back again to what I left.
Wake up
or I will be here again too soon
water flows into the bowl filling up to
flush down.
Then it fills again only to do it again.
Same bowl different crap.
If I am the water
I want to fill the cup, not the bowl
to hydrate the body to cleanse the soul.
It is time to wake up, to break the cycle,
to end the revolution.
I wake up and make my life a line.
From birth to death,
The next moment unknown.
I no longer will race back to a beginning
I know from an end I don't want.
The cycle repeats because of the
perceived comfort in knowing what is.

In knowing I can prepare for pain.
I embrace un-knowing.
I have no need for pain.
The revolution which just began, has
just ended.
It ended when I woke up.
I don't know what comes next
The cycle is broken.
I lovingly step into the moment to
embrace a loving un-known.
If a loving GOD is the force that set all
hearts to beating
And that heart beats with purpose
based on a foundation of love.
I have one prayer as I proceed with
passion
"Love's will be done"
I am awake.

I did

I did not choose the color of my skin.
I did not choose on my body what parts
stick out and what pokes in.
I did get to choose the me I am today.
what I'm gonna wear, how I'm gonna
act and what I'm gonna say.
Following the lead of parents and
teachers and mentors wise.
I fall down
I get up I keep my eyes on the prize.
My voice may be strong but need not be
loud.
My words, filled with truth do my
ancestors proud.
With trials and errors I've found my
style.
When you see my actions or hear my
words, I hope you smile.
I did not choose my height, my sex, my
skin.
I did choose to live fully in the skin I'm
in.

Alone

We enter this world alone. throughout
our lives we struggle not to remain that
way. searching for connection. seeking
partners to share our experiences.
whether we are successful or not we will
eventually leave as we entered, alone.

Cymatics

Life is the result of sound taking shape.
We are essentially the existence of
GOD's spoken word. We are not
listening for GOD to speak. We are
GOD's speech. Each of us is a complete
story. Our lives are not chapters in the
book of life. They are complete books. In
religion we are taught to listen to GOD.
We are taught to pray to GOD and wait
for a response. Life is that response. If
we are the spoken word of GOD then
GOD's response to us will come in
living form. GOD speaking to us will
not be a disembodied voice wafting out
of the ether. GOD speaks to us
constantly through the people, places
and things in our life.

Opposition

The opposite of love is fear not hate. In order to hate someone you must care for them, you must want better of them. In fearing we lose sight of any possibility of empathy or compassion from the other. In fear we forget the other is capable of love.

am I wrong?

Is it wrong to want to be loved?
I long to be loved. To be loved in the
same capacity which I give love. Am I
wrong to compare love? No one can
love the same as another, as no one can
think the same thought as another. My
destiny is to find a love so deep it's
bottom and top would be one. Yet from
the top you could not reach the bottom
and from the bottom one would never
attempt to reach the top. A love like a
rainbow - having no beginning and no
end - so incredibly beautiful it seems
unreal. Is it wrong to want to be loved?

Eros

from the moment our eyes met our
bodies began to synchronize into a
harmonic vibration.
When our heart beats became one it
took my breath away.
no other sound could be heard but us.
from that moment until the day I die I
will play second fiddle in this
symphony of love.

Truth

processing truth makes me cry. for there
is but one truth and it is not for me to
speak.
we have individual truths which is our
individual interpretations based on
perspective. for even in placing my
truth before you I must interpret my
view of this one truth. and in my
interpretation of this truth that is an
interpretation of "Love" the one truth, I
must sometimes remain silent. for in my
silences I speak truth.

Fault

at the rift of have and have not, want
and need, a quake begins.
from innocent infants we grow through
the tumultuous teens
on and on through the ages expanding
and contracting the chasm. sometimes
orgasmic sometimes destructive we
initiate the spasm. to find reason, for
expansion contraction, we counsel and
discuss unaware that this seismic fault is
us.

the pit

As I stand at the edge of this abyss
do I turn and walk away or jump and
take the risk?
is it fear that makes me stay?
is it fear that makes me run?
is if fear that makes me jump?
is it fear that makes me cry?
Is this truly living? if so, then why?
are there other options I must try?
in death there is so much certainty in life
there is simply why?
I stand at the edge with options before
me
and beside me
and behind me
In time my friend, you will know the
whole story.

Unlock

You hold the key to happiness. You
hold the key to joy. just holding the key
will not start a car, will not open a door,
will not unlock a lock.
We must partner our dreams, goals, and
desires with the key to accomplish
whatever it is we set out to accomplish.
We must take action.
Sometimes when you have the key but
don't know where it fits you must ask
for help. You may have to actually ask
for some assistance.
You may have to humble yourself. Yes,
you may find the solution on your own,
eventually. But there is no need to
postpone your happiness.
There is no need to postpone joy. Use
the keys that you were given at birth,
Use the keys you have picked up
throughout life to unlock and share.
Because the more you give of hope,
happiness, love and joy the more you
have to give. And the more you give the
more space you have to receive.

Wade in

I stand at the bank of the river of
creativity.
Where once there was a torrent now
there is nothing.
Where once I bathed luxuriously I now
long to slake my thirst.
Why am I here? Am I to despair over
loss?
There is meaning in the absence of what
I long for. As I reveled in the roar, the
flow, should I do the same in the quiet?
I long for the comfort of the cascades
that I have known.
I puzzle over a solution and in doing so
realize that I too am a piece to this
puzzle.

neo-activism

I am not a Black panther

or a member of SLA or Act Up or any
other.

Yet, I am changing the world.

This mornings actions consisted of
cooking an omelette, dressing a 5 year
old engaging an 8 year old and
encouraging a 12 year old.

I shape the future each day.

There is no need to race around outside
seeking windmills to charge.

Moments after waking it is clear what
need be done.

Sometimes the need wakes me in the
night.

I must comfort my future from the
nightmare that disrupts the now.

My activism is not a religious
movement, it is not a political position.

It is personal, it is persistent, it is
pressing.

My activism is parental.

Laughing

give in

lungs working like bellows

air going in to purify the blood

and rushing out sending pasta on a
fabulous flight across a living space

inhale refueling the fire roaring within,

unhinging the latch leaving loopiness to
prevail in a place where groundedness
can no longer take hold.

tears streaming down the face out of
place in this sea of ecstasy.

control is nowhere to be found and
momentarily unnecessary.

absurdity is the captain of this vessel
enabling snot to yo-yo from your
nostrils without care.

you the drunken cowboy in the bumper
car rodeo want it to stop so that soon
enough you can start again.

This day

Not every day is a special day.

Some days have to be 'the day before' or 'the day after'

and since yesterday was a good day, yeah just a good day, and tomorrow isn't here,

today is a special day.

My hopes and dreams are still alive today.

And there is weather and food.

And the people I love are close by.

Today is a special day.

I have a feeling about tomorrow, a good feeling.

But I'm gonna soak up today while it's here.

not everything has a name

it seems this rhyming couplet,

a product of my mind, that I've sublet

to a richer, stronger more passionate me.

a being I've kicked and fought and
grown to be.

contained within rhyme,

is a declaration of time

of position, of purpose, of meaning, of
action

set forth not by a warring, but a loving
faction.

we must not accept the wholesale
purchase of fear

instead let joy and purpose and hope
fall in our ear.

as moon goes round earth and earth
round sun

 it is time the greed and bloodshed be
done.

it has been done, set, established in time,

each two lines set down will rhyme,

and in an instance it stops.

We can make the same changes in the world around us.

It will take effort and thinking inside unfamiliar boxes.

This is how a revolution begins.

No longer accepting or coveting what we don't want.

It is time we burdened the world with our love.

It is time we shared a new way of thinking, of being.

Radical Thought: if we tell the producers of junk "We don't want it, We don't accept it and We don't buy".

They will be stuck with it.

Revolution is the solution.

It is not a revolt but a turn, a change.

Let us turn from what we don't want and turn to what we want.

Make a list, a real list, of that which you need,

Make sure the providers of product take heed.

In doing so you become the solution.

In doing so you begin the Revolution.

Honorific

I must cast aside these winter blues,

for softer, friendlier, warmer hues.

Infuriated by the daily news,

of inflated egos and skewed world views.

Of opinions formed with a narrow scope,

I must wake for this is dream, I hope.

Or do we really live where fear is king?

where loyal subjects bow down to nebulous thing.

I pluck my soul and like a bell I ring.

love and joy my soul does sing.

Filled to overflowing with GOD love radiation

I must broadcast like a radio station.

This is the moment, the now, the hour.

Like King Kong I must climb the tower,

to share a love from which I used to cower.

Yet now must broadcast, full power.

As opinions come and go and fade away,

this affirmation I make today.

I am filled with GOD's divine love, it is
my honor to share it with the world.

late winter

my blood moves through my veins like
jello
I am motivated to laze in places of
sunlight
I long to move like a sleek Italian sports
car on a German highway
instead of like a mini Cooper pulling a
camping trailer on the Garden State
Parkway.
until the warm arrives I must be
satisfied with passing time like a
cupcake through a camel instead of like
grease through a goose.
for now I can be found lounging where
the sun luxuriates and I will have a
longing look in my eyes
I will be waiting for spring to entice my
blood to flow freely once more

outside

Floating on the stream of consciousness

I discover reflected in my eyes

me, the me who I long to be

smothering the me that I despise

taking satisfaction in the action of not
waiting idly

aware without care of the me you
perceive of me.

my, my, my

Shamelessly I cast my eyes on what I want.

Undaunted I pursue a hope, a dream.

Yes, I question from time to time, yet not too often

If my reach exceeds my grasp, I must find a way to extend.

I may not be unique in not fully understanding

my value

my influence

my position

Each night I dream anew.

Each day I push aside fear and frustration clarifying the view.

Each step takes me further from all that I know.

For the moment I am here, right here.

I journey on, goal fixed in sight.

I move forward when awake and as I sleep at night.

Grasping what I want I thrust aside shame.

Fulfilling what I need is the beast I tame.

truce

by noticing I am not who I thought I
would be I come closer to being who I
should be. As I sit down to make sense
of it all I surrender to who I am.

druthers

love, sunshine, hope, dreams, passion,
companionship, love, joy, friendship.
just a few of the things I would rather
not do without.

Heavily ascending

lost inside of me

not wishing to be found

not lying in the clouds

or floating on the ground

buoyant in my hopes and dreams

not wanting to be found

the longer I remain

the more of me I'll know

how long can I stay here?

where else must I go?

all the doing has been done

all the work was no fun

discovering so much of me in me

the lottery, I think I've won

when I return to the world that
everyone calls real

I'm not sure what will happen, not
certain what I'll feel

I do know most definitely with new
eyes I will see

the wonderful amazing, the me inside of
me.

Spring

somewhere beneath the snow love and
hope and giggles feed the bulbs that
make the flowers grow. every today
brings us closer to spring when the sun
will shine to make the flowers sing.

Every thing

everything around me is inspiration to
create.

Perfection

what are the perfect words?

can one word express better than
another the emotion that I feel in a way
that is different to what another feels?

Or is my pain the same as your pain?

I search for self in the words I use to
describe myself. My search is not
because I am lost. It is more about
finding a true representation of me,
where I am.

In seeking these descriptors I am
amused by illustration of the complexity
of my complexion as I eye a complex
societal structure.

I know that makes no sense but it was
fun to write.

Words strung together, the pearls of
life's glorious necklace. I still strain to
find my words.

Words that describe this moment. For
should I search to find the words that
define me, in finding them I will change
me and need to renew my search to
define the new me.

I will find myself endlessly chasing the
tail of the dog that will end up being me
in the end.

academia

The following is as true as I can remember.

Two years of study at a college in my community.

My grades standing on their toes struggled to reach "D".

As far as I could see

a diploma was not to be.

Without matriculation would I have validation?

So I trained my body to do what I need,

and hoped my mind would take the seed.

Decades and continents, so many friends, so many faces.

My learning was in the world from these people from these places.

and oh, what I learned would not have come from the ivy-ed walls.

Information gained from back alleys, back streets and hawker stalls.

What semester would have trained me to see a fuller spectrum of light?

that my worth is not from validation but
birth right.

Each day continues my education,

for only I can issue my validation.

Purity

For thine is the kingdom of power and
glory. you may search for a million
lifetimes to find this place with your
eyes. yet should you seek it with your
heart and your soul you can find it in
only moments. for the kingdom of all
possibilities exist within you. the
acceptance of that which you already
own, the discovery of that which you
create will recognize you as the heir
apparent of this domain and the greatest
gift of all the universe will be yours.
Pure Joy.

do not wake me

I dream a wonderful dream. I don't
want to wake. There are dreams within
dreams and dreams within those
dreams each layered and interlaced.
Being aware of one layer makes me
aware of the other layers. Like the house
of mirrors I lose track of the original.
And like the house of mirrors I can
never see the original only the
reflections. When I eventually wake will
these three beautiful children remain?
Will all that I covet continue to exist?
How much of this world only exists in
my mind and how much is a universal
truth? I don't want answers. I don't
want the anxiety of knowing this will go
when I choose to un-blink. Regardless of
what the next moment holds for us I am
glad I dreamed you into my life. I am
glad I dreamed your love into my life.
Like a childhood toy that eventually
breaks, I will always have this even after
I wake.

(Autumn)

gliding over the earth greeted by the
crisp morning air. there is a freshness
about the day as I shamefully watch the
trees undressing. blood pumping
through me keeping me warm keeping
me moving. nothing can slow my
momentum as leaves crunch under foot.
then softness. what? no. the softness
muffles the crunch. each step sends a
scented unpleasantness aloft. I slide my
foot to release the scented surprise.
nature has softly spoken "enjoy as you
will, but this is mine".

honey

the cold has sunk in so far I have
forgotten my elasticity. I feel that I will
forever be locked in the shape that I am
in. from the dark recesses of the room I
am drawn into the pool of sunlight
haphazardly ambling through the south
facing windows. solar rays soak into
my skin unimpeded by three layers of
clothing. my muscles accept the
warmth. my body remembers it is more
than a solid. possibilities are illuminated
in my soul. like january honey I must
pour myself out of my chair for there is
much to do, much do be done, love to be
shared. thanks winter sun.

Home

this is the place where my longings find
no want to stray.

my heart beats without effort.

my dreams are refreshed, renewed.

where love flows from everything.

this is the port to which my ship must
return.

where I procrastinate out of
contentment.

from this place I need not wander.

if being here is work, I need not rest.

if I am a bird, this is my nest.

as whales swim the ocean

as word fill the poem

as I strive for excellence, this is my
home.

Another life

sleep

refresh, renew

to sleep is not to die

a glimpse into the what if, the wonder,
the why.

sleep

oxygen enriches the blood, enriches the
brain

creates a world with nothing mundane.

sleep

to live the life you wish for you

then wake and make that dream come
true.

Legacy

who tells the history of the conquered?

who speaks the story of the common man?

In one hundred years or one thousand will there be a story to tell?

what will be said? what will be read?

no one can say.

I strive to create a blip, a moment, a lasting impression.

It may be called art, from where I look it is just a part of me.

In a hundred years, a thousand or more may a part of me still resonate.

In a year or two or possibly five may who I am and what I do start conversations, foster discussion, warm a heart or cause a question.

I am a common man, not to be conquered.

I have tasks to do, a story to write, a life to live.

Indexed

when time has categorized, catalogued, indexed and shelved me

where is it that I will be found?

In the stone of existence how will my memory be etched?

Is the greatest significance of my being yet to come?

or has something I have done set in motion an event who's happening has already happened yet who's lasting impression has yet to be made?

will this life be just another leaf fallen in its time from the tree of life to be carried with the winds of time to collect among the others?

in decomposition will my definition be parsed?

or am I to fertilize one of more substance, more potential by the consumption of my parts?

or will I recede to the far reaches of the cosmos to shine brightly on other worlds? a star whose light so distant it never reaches this.

Boundary

halfway

neither fully here nor fully there.

in a space where the absence of things is
oppressive and confining at once.

color has contracted

to hide? to return? to renew?

in the space between what is real? what
is other?

can I trust what I think? In the thinking I
create that which is.

is there a moment, just as the runner
breaks the tape where I cross over from
here to now here.

remove the space from thinking and
now here becomes nowhere.

not quite halfway

not quite here not quite there.

I shout in my face, yet what I hear is the
reverberation of what I said not truly
the word flung from my mouth but the
chorus of all that have heard vibrating
with its essence.

if this is a circle then halfway is the
sweet spot.

the place within the all and any forward movement takes me closer to being without.

it is time to stop the silly questions.

it is time to repurpose doubt.

the silly smile appears when the realization of rhyme is heard.

seriously considering halfway is to seriously forget levity.

I sit I revel in the here. I revel in the hearing.

I will never be halfway until I know when the end is nearing.

Night stallion

the wind bears down like a train laden
with freight.

the gusts threaten my house of straw? of
wood? of stone?

worlds collide

the metaphysical, the theoretical, the
physical are one.

this is not the time of questioning, this is
the time of conjuring.

the dream is real.

I will not question whether I am awake
or deeper in sleep.

anything is possible.

I hang my hope on this peg of
possibilities fully knowing that
whatever I hang here is.

I will not push to dream harder

I will not push to fully awaken.

the winds erase the seam that separates
these worlds allowing all to fully live.

no matter which side of the coin I am
living, I am living.

the winds blow

not threatening to remove, not
threatening to erase

the winds blow air into my lungs giving
life to all that will be dreamed.

Ghost Dance

My reality is surprised to find there is Indian in my blood.

In my dreams I have known it there, yet in the waking world it was just a wish.

My heritage now has the power to propel me where it previously could only anchor me.

It is not this one puzzle piece which enables my release,

It is all the other pieces which have not been identified.

It is all the other pieces that represent the possibilities.

An unknown history that reshapes my future and generates an uncertain now.

Just like the angels unseen that positively influence my pursuits, my genetic recipe flavors my living.

I am the Indian, the African, the Spaniard, the Witch, the Shaman, the Herbalist, the Dreamer, the Magician, the on and on.

I need not identify the individual items that combine to become me I must honor the me they have become.

Holiness has made me think and
rethink. all that could come from
holiness inside my think is: we are one.

Shine

Oh baby, I see the light. from birth it has
been, but I could not see.

the magnificent amazing inside of me.

I needed to grow. I needed to live. I
needed to love. I needed to be.

now I can see it. now it is clear.

my heart is open I'm ready to hear.

It is me. I am the one I have been
waiting for.

I release me. I open all windows and the
door.

I conjure magic with power universal.

a power so strong now that I've washed
my soul.

I have bathed in the divine and I accept
it is time. It is my time, yes, my time, my
time to shine.

Organic farming

We are all farmers

not necessarily good ones

not always aware of our crops

applications filled out

goals set

kind words spoken

we are not always aware of the seeds we plant

we are not always aware of how and when we tend our crops

hopefully we are aware of our harvest

help is given

job secured

kindness received

love overflowing, joy in abundance.

humanity

the body of GOD is fractured and we
are its pieces. the big bang that caused
this rift has robbed us of fully
remembering our oneness. we connect
with others of similar purpose. we repel
others whose purpose does not align.
we long for each other. we need each
other. we grow and harvest frustration
when we, the pieces of this complex
puzzle, do not fit. one day we will know
wholeness again. today we give thanks
for the journey. may it continue for
some time.

Outside in

Outside dormant trees grow restless to wake

swaying with underlying agitation in the wind.

Inside ten or more voices vie for attention tempting me to venture toward folly, toward the unknown, toward uncertainty.

As the world wears its winter blanket hinting that it soon will wake,

the future perks my curiosity. I risk my identity. I risk my sanity.

The earth risks nothing, it accepts the chilling cold as it welcomes the searing heat. Its extremes in balance.

I accept my confusion, the illusion of knowledge, of power.

Am I a sentient cancer cell struggling to thrive on this entity?

Are we purposefully balanced? this planet and this person.

My purpose must be greater than to gratify my person.

My actions must be greater than to enjoy existence.

Outside all that is necessary to sustain me harmoniously coexists, perpetually revolving the cycle of life.

Inside I struggle to exist to honor that which is greater than me yet positions itself to nurture me.

I let the inside out so that the outside may fill within making the inner as great as the outer.

Freedom

I un-trap myself from the thoughts of
others. I unbind myself from me.
releasing the bonds that allow me to be
less than fully me I step into the world
of infinite possibilities. my mind is free
to think a new strategy of being, that
celebrates the me I am. Un-bound from
color, sex, age, religion I become you
and in doing so discover me. Un-
tethered I am able to see you in me and
therefore see me in the eyes of every
you. by fully accepting me I do not
separate myself from all others but
become fully united in the body human.
by doing so I create a most positive
loving now, enveloping the universe.

undulate

the gravity of life bears heavier on my
soul, each day. I strengthen my resolve
to carry the tune, the melody of my life,
as the increased weight tugs at the notes
in their suspension. I sing. the birds
dismiss gravity and fly. the bees shun
the science that restricts them to
pedestrians. I too will defy. find the
gaps of weightlessness. attach myself to
the ideas as they soar. releasing the
tangible to attach to the unfathomable.
as kelp in the universal ocean I stretch
upward belying the density that is.
understanding the insistence of the
current yet staying true to an un-plotted
course. neither lost nor found I overflow
with hope squeezed from my conjuring
by life's gravity.

march

There are decisions to be made. Will you suffer this or will you experience it? Decisions to be made, victim, participant, enabler, spectator, controller. This is your life. You set the rules. You pick the direction. The emotions you display belong to you, come from you. There are decisions to be made. This is your life. Beat that drum however you like. This is your parade.

tick - tock

no matter whether I stop and think or rush ahead, it keeps going. I tried making it. I can't buy it. Sometimes I am living on borrowed allotments of it. there are moments when I feel like I have been here before. there are moments when I no longer want to be here. since I am here and this is now, I guess this is my time.

the present

He looked to the heavens and asked,
"For me? What shall I do with it?. After
a long pause GOD replied "Do what you
will with it, Life is my gift to you.

lineage

I look up to my father and over to my
son.

so many many dreams we have begun.

my father looks to me and my son looks
to his dad.

expectations to be reached or missed

good times to be had.

one day we will be gone and three more
in our place.

what will they think of us before the
memories are erased.

Boundaries

in the room with no walls we find
ourselves.

each of us has been drawn here from
points unknown throughout the
universe.

this is our destination yet this is not our
purpose.

of our many crafts, we weave words to
comfort, to enlighten, to entertain, to
amuse, to heal.

sometimes all at once.

we will, in time, pass that which we
have gained on to the next.

this passing along of our treasure is
what is meant to happen.

that which we search to find we will
never see.

that which we pass along we will never
know.

yet we give thanks for the ability to seek
and share and receive.

what we should never know is that we
are the miracle to others.

unknowing of this, we continue.

amidst

somewhere between here and there. I
am fully aware of where I am not. and
yet here I am, suspended between my
goals and my fears.

pot of gold

fortune has dropped so much
wonderful into my life. some of it I have
worked for. some have been
unexpected. Gifts. I have deserved it all
which has taken some time to believe.
the life I live is truly awesome. so many
people have entered my life and given
me inspiration. I give thanks for my
ability to dream. I give thanks for the
ability to bring so many dreams into
reality. when you look at this, my life, it
is not lucky. this is blessed.

Nothing

Some mornings there is just nothing.

nothing to motivate or inspire and
nothing to discourage.

No want or need for more.

The nothing has no color yet when I
think of nothing it is gray.

Nothing is not a room or a place. It is no
place. It is the absence of all I know.

It is the unknown, the unknowable

neither comfortable nor threatening.

soundless and un-seeking a vibrational
signature

within the nothing I seek the sound of
my heartbeat, my breath, my footfalls.

I seek the comfort of me, not the doing
me, the being me.

soul food

fruitless task? you ask.

my answer:

The plant un-nurtured will bear no fruit.

Well tended this plant may produce
more

to eat, to sustain me is what I do this for.

That which is plucked from this vine
cannot be deposited in a bank or
purchase a car, a bus, a tank.

It is devoured sustaining the heart
encouraging the mind

making the now worthwhile, somehow.

This crop remains unseen by most

feeds the spirit.

Soul food I grow

a proclamation, not a boast.

Young lady

Young lady

I look you in the eye

not because you are the object of desire

it is not that you set my heart, my mind, my loin on fire

I nod to you

It is my bow

to the honor you are born with but may not know right now

it is not the curve of your hip

or the pucker of your lip that catches my eye

It is the Queen in you

the hope that one day you will be president

the hope that one day you will know your power

Young lady

I look you in the eye and see a daughter, a sister, a mother, a grandmother

and hope you do not know their struggle

Young lady

my hope that should you choose so in
this life

you accomplish more than just wife

you turn from me and laugh

you think your underwire ignites my
fire

that your hip makes my heart beat dip

Young lady

I look you in the eye

and send to you via spiritual wifi

honor, courage, strength and love

for with this, the girl you are

will become the lady I see.

Young black man

I wave at you

not because we are friends

although we may be one day

because not very long ago you were
unseen

not very long ago you could not grow to
be a man

you could only be a boy

Young black man

I nod to you

because maybe your father

or your father's father was worth only
the work he could do

and you are worth my time

Young black man

you see me and laugh

you see my nod and don't understand

may you never know

I wave at me in you

the me that did not know hate

the me that did not know injustice

the me that did not know I was not a
leading man

the me that did not know what was
ahead

Young black man

one day you will wave at me

when you wave I hope you wave at you
inside of me.

Black Friday

Today is black Monday or Tuesday or
Wednesday.
Everyday is black day.
Although I have tried, I have never been
un-black.
I have been told it is okay to be
overwhelmed by being me.
Thus making it okay to be my own
burden.
I am black.
Yes, I can dance, I just can't dance out of
my skin.
I have tried, to be less black for this
interview, to be more black for that
crowd.
I have bleached my hair.
I can not bleach my soul.
I have wrestled with myself, only to
stop when considering who the winner
will be.
I must unburden myself of the burden
that I am a burden.
I must dance into my skin, dance into
my soul.
I must, by loving me, let others know
how to love me.
Today is Black Friday, My Friday.
Today is the day I stop bearing the
overwhelming burden of being me.
Today I stop being only black and start

being all black.
Today is when being fully me helps you
be fully you.
Today is Black Friday. Tomorrow is
Black Saturday.
Each day will begin black and end
black.
Forever it will be that way.

I am Black history

From Africa to America spanning the world, quite possibly

my DNA struggled to survive to make me.

My existence is a testament to survival fitness

my life is to nurture the future and to bear witness the past.

My name is the name that to property they gave.

My heritage my lineage is that of a slave

Yes, slave, property harsh words to hear

Great Granddad was born enslaved, three generations too near.

Granddad laid bricks played music and sang

Hope from Grandma's illiterate lips, I sprang

A lineage broken in Georgia or Carolina south

passed on and on by word of mouth.

The legacy must pass through me to give my children power

for their momma's line stepped off the Mayflower.

in both I must help them see honor

for the strength and the pride that made
me must endure.

listening and teaching and learning I
press on without blame.

learning from the past about my past, I
move on without shame.

Each new day, new creation I write the
story

one of survival, renewal, reflection
doggedly pushing toward glory

I am black yesterday, I am black now. I
am black history.

I never

I may never be voted most sexy

not being most popular is alright by me.

To have tried my hardest and not to win
is well...

Okay, I need to stop.

All lies.

I would like to know that my caring and
kindness makes me popular.

It would be nice to know that someone
covets me from afar.

Oh how I would frivolously spend my
lottery winnings throwing money to
help others and grinning.

My heart may not be pure but my
intentions are good.

I will accept the burdens of fame and
wealth,

yet not at the expense of my family or
their health.

Maybe I am not to have these.

for my terms the givers are not pleased.

So I may not be most sexy, most
popular, most wealthy.

I am happy, I am loved, I am healthy.

Ordinary

It is funny that ordinary is not quite so

for each of us has a unique ordinary
which makes it less than common

my routine is not your routine, yet we
each have a routine which becomes our
norm and so our days become alike
because our status quo stays just so.

which makes extra ordinary just, normal
to a degree.

If one is extraordinary day in and day
out then the extra becomes ordinary.

my way is unlike any other way yet
every day I do things my way.

unique you say, oh, on the contrary

this is just my ordinary.

Soliloquy

I shout at the sky.

Will I get GOD's attention? Am I significant?

I do not wait for the answer.

I am worthy.

I have done my fair share and can see no end in sight.

I am worthy I repeat, not necessarily to be heard but to hear myself.

The words fall out effortlessly yet I propel them to go further.

I launch them to go beyond just my ears.

I shout at the ground for maybe my words will rebound skyward where GOD will hear.

I must speak these words.

I know not what I say.

The words give me purpose. The words give me meaning.

I am worthy.

With one more utterance I may begin to believe.

With one more shout I may accept that when I can hear it GOD can hear it.

Pain

The result of toil and wear has born in me a parasitic presence that feeds on my soul.

Constantly it gnaws on hope and joy.

Eroding all but the want of its departure.

wearing away, wearing away.

I long for its absence.

A moments rest.

I would accept nothing, if it meant being devoid of this.

Simplicity no longer exists.

This parasite has attached itself to simple, making it anything but.

Who was I before? Will I ever be again?

You are not my friend. Go away.

Your presence does not make me stronger. Go away.

Only in your absence will I be stronger.

I could use that strength to fight you now.

As silently as you arrived, will you please leave?

drought

I stand at the bank of the river of creativity. where once there was a torrent now there is nothing. where once I bathed luxuriously I now long to slake my thirst. why am I here? am I to despair over loss? there is meaning in the absence of what I long for. as I reveled in the roar, the flow, should I do the same in the quiet? I long for the comfort of the cascades that I have known. I puzzle over a solution and in doing so realize that I too am a piece to this puzzle.

Fault

at the rift of have and have not, want
and need, a quake begins.

from innocent infants we grow

through the tumultuous teens

on and on through the ages

expanding and contracting the chasm.

sometimes orgasmic sometimes
destructive

we initiate the spasm.

to find reason, for expansion
contraction, we counsel and discuss

unaware that this seismic fault is us.

Frustration

Things are prepared and do not go as planned.

Moments are lost for no reason.

He stops speaking to you.

what have you said? What have you done?

No matter how much you plead the answers don't come.

A tear forms, teeters on the edge threatening to spill over the lid to slide carefree down my face. A tear that threatens to betray my calm composed exterior.

Internally temperature rises.

The outside stays cool not flashing signs of anything. Composure.

Expectations weren't met.

The results in no way represent the preparation.

She won't look at you.

My face is numb. My heart races on.

My lungs have been filled with cotton, or so it seems.

This has a name. You wish you were good with names. I wish I were good with names.

I want to remember this name. I want to name this.

I swear. I swear, again. I hate to swear.

Whatever this is, is making me swear.

No. Making me do things I don't like doing.

This isn't me.

Wait, I know its name.

Now it's gone.

Unlock

You hold the key to happiness. You hold the key to joy.

just holding the key will not start a car,

will not open a door,

will not unlock a lock.

We must partner our dreams, goals, and desires with the key to accomplish whatever it is we set out to accomplish.

We must take action.

Sometimes when you have the key but don't know where it fits you must ask for help. You may have to actually ask for some assistance.

You may have to humble yourself.

Yes, you may find the solution on your own, eventually.

But there is no need to postpone your happiness.

There is no need to postpone joy.

Use the keys that you were given at birth,

Use the keys you have picked up throughout life to unlock and share.

Because the more you give of hope,
happiness, love and joy

the more you have to give.

And the more you give the more space
you have to receive.

truth

processing truth makes me cry. for there is but one truth and it is not for me to speak. we have individual truths which is our individual interpretations based on perspective. for even in placing my truth before you I must interpret my view of this one truth. and in my interpretation of this truth that is an interpretation of "Love" the one truth, I must sometimes remain silent. for in my silences I speak truth.

unlovable

I sit in the shadow of earth

unlovable?

as I try to love I trample hope

my past hurt becomes my today hurt

I want to love you so purely so deeply

I want you to love me back

outside the rain cleanses the world

inside my blood thickens with want

as I see, I want to be seen

by you.

I can only hope that we choose
separately and together

we choose to walk out of the shadows to
see each other not as we want to see
each other but as we need each other to
see.

we have had moments

and I want as many more moments as I
can get

I selfishly want moments that make us
both resonate with joy from the soul

you are worth it as I too am worth it.

Grand Canyon

As I stand at the edge of this abyss
do I turn and walk away or jump and
take the risk?
is it fear that makes me stay?
is it fear that makes me run?
is if fear that makes me jump?
is it fear that makes me cry?
Is this truly living? if so then why?
are there other options I must try?
in death there is so much certainty
in life there is simply why?
I stand at the edge with options before
me

and beside me

and behind me
In time my friend, you will know the
whole story.

her

The fresh smell of her hair as I hold her close. That moment when our heart beats synch. Inhaling air that is infused with her essence. The sensation of her muscles tensing and relaxing in my hands. The electricity transferred as a part of me brushes a part of her. It is not being in love that I desire. It is being in love with her that intoxicates me.

"You ignite me!!"

I want to love you as fully as I can theoretically, metaphysically, emotionally, physically. I have previously loved you selfishly to fill a hole somewhere in my torso. I want and need to love you to feed the fire in my soul.

wanting

Is it wrong to want to be loved?

I long to be loved. To be loved in the same capacity which I give love. Am I wrong to compare love? No one can love the same as another, as no one can think the same thought as another. My destiny is to find a love so deep it's bottom and top would be one. Yet from the top you could not reach the bottom and from the bottom one would never attempt to reach the top. A love like a rainbow - having no beginning and no end - so incredibly beautiful it seems unreal. Is it wrong to want to be loved?

Look

Staring at the source of creativity I am compelled to look away.

The source emits a persistent pulse to produce,

not suggestively but emphatically.

The immenseness of this singularity initiates from a single subatomic particle.

It is not a complex chemical, it is the root of all.

It is pure and can not be purer.

To gaze upon it is so bitter-sweet,

For if everything has a beginning then it must have an end.

Which means that at some point I must look away.

At some point I will no longer be within the gaze of this.

Wind

From where do you come?

no one seems to question the wind.

it either is or it isn't.

yet we as a species struggle with GOD.

what generates wind?

not the stirred air of a fan.

not the gust of a closing door.

what makes that which blows the leaves
from the trees?

what makes that which wreaks havoc in
the trailer park?

we accept that wind happens

we don't question why.

we don't question how.

we do question an energy greater than
us.

I guess this question of wind can be
scientifically reasoned and we wholesale
accept those reasons.

we accept that someone smarter than us
has made sense of it.

if we did not accept the science and fully
searched for an answer our brains
would probably explode.

I do not question the wind. I ponder the wind.

for as long as there is wind anything can happen.

for if this thing that can not be contained or fully explained and conjures itself into a half existence can have a tangible and lasting effect.

Then, anything is possible.

work

in the place where I work

hope greets you at the door

your fears can be placed in a box in the corner

impossible just does not feel at home

magic happens

miracles occur

friends are made

physical limitations are pushed

amazing moments are created and recreated

everyone is encouraged to fully be who they are

life is lived

resurrection

I died 5 years ago

the moment I let doubt overshadow hope

when I stopped believing that which I am was 'enough'

and started accepting "I need do more".

I stopped breathing.

When I started listening to my ego

and stopped following my heart

it slowed at first, then it stopped beating.

Consumed by keeping up with the Jones's (whoever they are)

I stopped dreaming.

There is food on the table but my soul stopped feeding years ago.

The shame is no one misses me.

No one misses what I did not do because it was not expected to be done.

No one knew that I was the one

the one who conjures the miracles

Unseen miracles are not missed.

I miss me.

As of today I stop doing what is expected of me.

Today I return to the place I died,

to the place I remain unmoving.

I have found the courage to breathe life into me.

We need, Hell, I need me to bring back the miracles.

I need me to once again close my eyes and see that doing things is not living life.

I died 5 years ago.

Today I resurrect me.

William Forchion

ABOUT THE AUTHOR

William Forchion, the youngest of three kids, grew up on a small farm in Hammonton, NJ with enough space to wonder and dream. As an adult William has been able to breathe life into many of his dreams. Having struggled with reading growing up William credits his high school English teachers and Acting teacher with planting the seeds of possibility that grew into his writing. William hopes to pass on his dream embodiment to everyone he encounters. William lives in Brattleboro, Vermont where he is a father to three wonderful kids.

You can find out more at:

www.billforchion.com

William Forchion

www.ingramcontent.com/pod-product-compliance
Lightning Source LLC
Chambersburg PA
CBHW031323040426
42443CB00005B/193